Your Government:
How It Works

The Presidency

Kevin J. McNamara

Arthur M. Schlesinger, jr.
Senior Consulting Editor

Chelsea House Publishers
Philadelphia

To Hilary and Whitney

CHELSEA HOUSE PUBLISHERS
Editor in Chief Stephen Reginald
Production Manager Pamela Loos
Art Director Sara Davis
Director of Photography Judy L. Hasday
Managing Editor James D. Gallagher
Senior Production Editor LeeAnne Gelletly

Staff for THE PRESIDENCY
Project Editor/Publishing Coordinator Jim McAvoy
Associate Art Director Takeshi Takahashi
Series Designer Takeshi Takahashi, Keith Trego

The Chelsea House World Wide Web address is
http://www.chelseahouse.com

First Printing
1 3 5 7 9 8 6 4 2

Library of Congress Cataloging-in-Publication Data

McNamara, Kevin J.
    The presidency / by Kevin J. McNamara
        p. cm. — (Your government—how it works)
    Includes bibliographical references and index.
    Summary: Discusses the history, duties, powers, and traditions of the office of the president and how presidents from Washington to Clinton have handled crises during their terms in office.
    ISBN 0-7910-5533-7 (hc)
    1. Presidents—United States—Juvenile literature. [1. Presidents.
    2. United States—Politics and government.] I. Title. II. Series.

JK517 .M36 2000
973'.09'9—dc21   99-048608

Contents

Introduction

Government: Crises of Confidence

Arthur M. Schlesinger, jr.

FROM THE START, Americans have regarded their government with a mixture of reliance and mistrust. The men who founded the republic understood the importance of government. "If men were angels," observed the 51st Federalist Paper, "no government would be necessary." But men are not angels. Because human beings are subject to wicked as well as to noble impulses, government was deemed essential to assure freedom and order.

The American revolutionaries, however, also knew that government could become a source of injury and oppression. The men who gathered in Philadelphia in 1787 to write the Constitution therefore had two purposes in mind: They wanted to establish a strong central authority and to limit that central authority's capacity to abuse its power.

To prevent the abuse of power, the Founding Fathers wrote two basic principles into the Constitution. The principle of federalism divided power between the state governments and the central authority. The principle of the separation of powers subdivided the central authority itself into three branches—the executive, the legislative, and the judiciary—so that "each may be a check on the other."

YOUR GOVERNMENT: HOW IT WORKS examines some of the major parts of that central authority, the federal government. It explains how various officials, agencies, and departments operate and explores the political organizations that have grown up to serve the needs of government.

Introduction

The federal government as presented in the Constitution was more an idealistic construct than a practical administrative structure. It was barely functional when it came into being.

This was especially true of the executive branch. The Constitution did not describe the executive branch in any detail. After vesting executive power in the president, it assumed the existence of "executive departments" without specifying what these departments should be. Congress began defining their functions in 1789 by creating the Departments of State, Treasury, and War.

President Washington, assisted by Secretary of the Treasury Alexander Hamilton, equipped the infant republic with a working administrative structure. Congress also continued that process by creating more executive departments as they were needed.

Throughout the 19th century, the number of federal government workers increased at a consistently faster rate than did the population. Increasing concerns about the politicization of public service led to efforts—bitterly opposed by politicians—to reform it in the latter part of the century.

The 20th century saw considerable expansion of the federal establishment. More importantly, it saw growing impatience with bureaucracy in society as a whole.

The Great Depression during the 1930s confronted the nation with its greatest crisis since the Civil War. Under Franklin Roosevelt, the New Deal reshaped the federal government, assigning it a variety of new responsibilities and greatly expanding its regulatory functions. By 1940, the number of federal workers passed the 1 million mark.

Critics complained of big government and bureaucracy. Business owners resented federal regulation. Conservatives worried about the impact of paternalistic government on self-reliance, on community responsibility, and on economic and personal freedom.

When the United States entered World War II in 1941, government agencies focused their energies on supporting the war effort. By the end of World War II, federal civilian employment had risen to 3.8 million. With peace, the federal establishment declined to around 2 million in 1950. Then growth resumed, reaching 2.8 million by the 1980s.

A large part of this growth was the result of the national government assuming new functions such as: affirmative action in civil rights, environmental protection, and safety and health in the workplace.

Some critics became convinced that the national government was a steadily growing behemoth swallowing up the liberties of the people. The 1980s brought new intensity to the debate about government growth. Foes of Washington bureaucrats preferred local government, feeling it more responsive to popular needs.

But local government is characteristically the government of the locally powerful. Historically, the locally powerless have often won their human and constitutional rights by appealing to the national government. The national government has defended racial justice against local bigotry, upheld the Bill of Rights against local vigilantism, and protected natural resources from local greed. It has civilized industry and secured the rights of labor organizations. Had the states' rights creed prevailed, perhaps slavery would still exist in the United States.

Americans are still of two minds. When pollsters ask large, spacious questions—Do you think government has become too involved in your lives? Do you think government should stop regulating business?—a sizable majority opposes big government. But when asked specific questions about the practical work of government—Do you favor Social Security? Unemployment compensation? Medicare? Health and safety standards in factories? Environmental protection?—a sizable majority approves of intervention.

We do not like bureaucracy, but we cannot live without it. We need its genius for organizing the intricate details of our daily lives. Without bureaucracy, modern society would collapse. It would be impossible to run any of the large public and private organizations we depend on without bureaucracy's division of labor and hierarchy of authority. The challenge is to keep these necessary structures of our civilization flexible, efficient, and capable of innovation.

More than 200 years after the drafting of the Constitution, Americans still rely on government but also mistrust it. These attitudes continue to serve us well. What we mistrust, we are more likely to monitor. And government needs our constant attention if it is to avoid inefficiency, incompetence, and arbitrariness. Without our informed participation, it cannot serve us individually or help us as a people to attain the lofty goals of the Founding Fathers.

Faced with the divided opinions of his advisors and Congress, President John F. Kennedy had to make the final decision on how America would respond to the Cuban Missile Crisis.

CHAPTER **1**

War, Crises, and the U.S. Constitution

IT WAS A MORNING like any other in the White House that October when one of America's youngest presidents, John F. Kennedy, still wearing his morning robe, reading the newspapers, and drinking his coffee, was interrupted by an aide. The aide had alarming news—Russia had begun to place large missiles in Cuba, an island off the coast of Florida, in order to fire nuclear weapons at the United States.

What would the president do?

President Kennedy brought his advisors together to ask them what they thought he should do. The advisors didn't agree with each other and argued among themselves. Some urged the president to attack Cuba and destroy the missiles. Others warned that Russia would respond with its own attack on the United States, starting a major war.

The president then turned to the Congress, which shares with the president the responsibility for war and peace. He asked the senior

A United States naval destroyer blockading the Cuban coast intercepts the Soviet freighter Ivan Polzunov *during the Cuban Missile Crisis in 1962.*

members of Congress for their advice, but they also disagreed with each other on what should be done.

The question, however, kept coming—from demanding reporters, nervous soldiers, baffled government officials, and frightened Americans everywhere: "President Kennedy, what will you do to protect us?"

Only the president could decide what America would do, and so he decided.

To prevent Russia from shipping to Cuba the final parts needed to arm the missiles and aim them at the United States, President Kennedy surrounded the island with U.S. Navy warships, and told the Russians to keep their ships away. If the Russian ships were to try to get past this blockade, the U.S. ships would blow them up. The president then appeared on television to explain his decision to the American people and to warn them that war was likely—perhaps a nuclear war—if Russian ships tried to force their way through the U.S. naval blockade of Cuba.

America waited. The Russian ships continued to sail toward Cuba, directly into the loaded gun barrels of the

U.S. Navy's warships. President Kennedy ordered American soldiers to prepare for war. The whole world held its breath.

"His hand went up to his face and covered his mouth," one adviser said of the president at this time. "He opened and closed his fist. His face seemed drawn, his eyes pained, almost gray. We stared at each other across the table."

Finally came the message that the Russian ships "stopped dead in the water." War had been avoided; and the missiles would be removed from Cuba.

This true story, which is known as the Cuban Missile Crisis of 1962, demonstrates why the office of the president was created. Groups of people will disagree on what action to take, especially under a threat of war or some other crisis. Yet a whole nation of people must act quickly and confidently at these times in order to protect itself.

The people who created the presidency learned this lesson from their reading of history, from their personal experience in fighting the British in the Revolutionary War, and from the crises that arose when they tried to manage their new country, the United States, without a president. Wars and other crises, therefore, gave birth to the presidency, and these kinds of events continue to determine how important presidents are and how much power they have.

The office of the U.S. president was created by a document known as the United States **Constitution,** which also created all other parts of the original government of the United States. The two other major government agencies are the Congress (which has two parts: the House of Representatives and the Senate), and the judiciary (which is made up of judges, the most important of whom sit on the United States Supreme Court). The Constitution also established America's most important laws, which are the rules that the president and all other Americans must follow.

After America declared its independence from Great Britain in 1776 and then defeated the British army in the Revolutionary War, Americans won the freedom to govern themselves. Throughout most of the 1780s, the 13 original colonies—Connecticut, Delaware, Georgia, Maryland, Massachusetts, New Hampshire, New Jersey, New York, North Carolina, Pennsylvania, Rhode Island, South Carolina, and Virginia—cooperated with each other under an agreement called the Articles of Confederation.

Under this weak central government, however, the former colonies remained largely separate and independent from one another. The U.S. government, for example, could not collect taxes directly from the people, nor could it force the former colonies to pay for the costs of the central government. The government also could not force them to obey the treaties—or agreements—it signed with other nations.

In an attempt to fix these weaknesses, 55 men representing all 13 of the former colonies met at Independence Hall in Philadelphia in 1787 to create a new agreement that would help them work more closely together. This meeting led to a new and stronger organization, or government. These men wrote and approved the Constitution, then con-

Independence Hall, in Philadelphia, Pennsylvania. The presidency was created here when the Founding Fathers wrote the United States Constitution.

vinced a majority of the former colonies to accept the Constitution, thereby creating the United States of America. These leaders of the new nation became known as the Founding Fathers.

The Founding Fathers created the office of the president because a single person can do certain things better than can the other two branches of government created by the Constitution. Those two branches, the Congress and the Judiciary, are groups of people—members of Congress and judges—who take the time to think about and discuss problems. Only after usually lengthy discussion, do they try to solve a problem by getting a majority of their members to agree on a solution. Even then, these solutions must follow certain rules. As an individual, on the other hand, a president can make decisions more easily, respond more quickly to events, and handle a crisis better when it first appears. Presidents are better able to enforce the laws, can deal better with other nations, and can do and say things secretly when that is required.

Like a king or queen, the American president is recognized as the head of state, which means he is seen as a symbol of the United States and its citizens. Indeed, the

One of the responsibilities of a head of state is receiving and entertaining important foreign guests. President Bill Clinton (left), with England's Queen Elizabeth II (center), and Prince Philip (right). The Constitution's separation of powers makes it impossible for the U. S. president to be all-powerful.

president is the only public official elected by all Americans. Although American adult voters cast votes for their choice for president, 538 presidential electors in what is called the electoral college formally elect the president. The candidate who wins the greatest number of votes in a state wins all of that state's electoral votes. Each state gets a number of electoral votes in proportion to its size. Following the popular election, the presidential electors gather in their state capitals, cast their votes—usually in accordance with the popular vote—and the results are then sent to Washington D.C. to be counted by the Congress.

As the chief executive, the president is in charge of the **cabinet**—the leaders of the departments of government, such as the attorney general and secretary of state. He also manages the entire executive branch of government, such as the Departments of Justice and Agriculture, and agencies such as the Environmental Protection Agency (EPA) and the Federal Bureau of Investigation (FBI). As a political leader, the president directs the national operations of his political party—whether he is a Republican or Democrat—and leads the members of Congress who belong to the same party.

The Constitution also gives the president the power to make treaties with other nations as well as to appoint U.S. ambassadors to other nations, to choose members of his cabinet, and to appoint the judges who are in charge of U.S. federal—but not state—courts. Finally, the Constitution also makes the president the commander in chief of the armed forces: the Army, Air Force, Navy, and Marines.

America's Founding Fathers created the office of the president reluctantly. They had blamed King George III of England for behaving like a dictator, which forced them to fight the Revolutionary War. This war quickly became a fight against not only England and King George but against the very idea of a king. Thus, after the war, many of the Founding Fathers feared that a powerful president would turn into the equivalent of a king.

As a result, they limited the president's power in many ways. They divided the government into separate organizations, which had the effect of separating the government's powers. Only Congress can pass new laws, for instance, but only federal judges can decide whether a new law obeys the Constitution, the highest law. Presidents usually sign new laws that they are in favor of, but they can **veto** (reject) a new law they do not like. Congress can overrule a president's veto (enact the law without the president's approval) if the members of Congress vote once again for the new law, this time with two-thirds of the members of Congress voting "yes." This **separation of powers** makes it impossible for a president to be all-powerful, like a king or dictator. In this and other ways, the Congress, the presidency, and the judiciary can each stop the others from disobeying the law or exercising too much power over the people.

The Constitution places additional limits on a president's power. An individual can serve as president for only two consecutive four-year terms and can be removed from office by the process of **impeachment,** which is like a trial conducted by the Congress. Only two presidents—Andrew Johnson and William Jefferson Clinton—have been impeached, or charged with crimes, by the House of Representatives. The Senate convicted neither man. President Richard Nixon resigned in 1974 when a House committee began the process of impeaching him as a result of the Watergate scandal.

Despite these rules, presidents have not always found the guidance they needed from the Constitution. As a result, the individuals who served as president sometimes were required to create their own rules. In addition, wars, the threat of wars, and other crises have increased the power of the presidency over time.

R. Veenfliet.

George Washington assumed command of the Continental army in 1775. Washington's leadership during the Revolution led to his election as the first United States president.

CHAPTER 2

The Founding Fathers and the Presidency:
George Washington to John Quincy Adams

KNOWN AS "the father of our country," George Washington did more than any other person to create the office of the president. As the general who led Americans to victory over the British in the Revolutionary War, Washington was a hero. Elected to serve as the presiding officer at the Constitutional Convention in Philadelphia, Washington influenced how the Founding Fathers wrote the Constitution. After Washington was elected as the first U.S. president and started working at his new job in 1789, he sometimes found no guidelines in the Constitution to tell him what he should do. This forced Washington to create some informal rules, or traditions, which presidents still follow.

Presidents, for instance, are elected to four-year terms, according to the Constitution. However, the Constitution originally did not limit the number of terms a president could serve. Because President Washington decided to retire after only two terms, he created a tradition, or unofficial rule, that was followed by all other presidents, until Franklin Roosevelt won a third term in 1940. Later, Congress passed the 22nd Amendment (or change) to the Constitution to require all presidents to follow George Washington's example and serve only two terms.

George Washington also played a big role in deciding where the nation's capital would be located. New York City was the nation's first capital, then Philadelphia became the capital. A decision was made in 1790, however to locate the capital on the Potomac River on land donated by Maryland and Virginia. In this way, the capital would be placed midway between the North and the South, the two major regions that had always seen themselves as different.

President Washington also started the tradition of bringing together the leaders of the most important departments of the executive branch of government as the president's cabinet. The president appoints members of the cabinet, but the most important of them must also be approved by the U.S. Senate. Washington's first cabinet consisted of only four individuals. Because the size of the government has grown, today there are about a dozen cabinet members.

Washington delivered the first inaugural speech at his **inauguration,** the ceremony during which the person who has been elected officially takes the oath of office. Washington also delivered the first **state of the union message.** Although the Constitution requires this annual report by the president to Congress, it was George Washington who decided to appear in person before Congress to read his message, a tradition that continues to this day. Washington's best-known speech was his farewell address, in which he warned Americans against getting involved in the conflicts among the European nations. Though the farewell address did not become as strong a tradition among presidents, Washington's fear of involvement with Europe would be shared by future presidents and would shape America's early history.

Indeed, America's relationship with France was the first major issue to divide the young nation, a division that led to the creation of the first political parties. Two members of Washington's own cabinet—Secretary of State Thomas Jefferson and Secretary of the Treasury Alexander Hamilton—led the opposing parties. By the time Washington's **vice president,** John Adams, was elected in 1796 as America's second president, Adams, Hamilton, and their followers became known as the Federalists. Jefferson and his followers became known as the Democratic-Republicans.

During the Adams administration, the possibility of war with France created a controversy between the Federalists, who supported President Adams, and the Democratic-Republicans, who favored France. President Adams tried to silence his critics with the Alien and Sedition Acts of 1798, which attempted to limit the political activities of Frenchmen in America and to silence Jeffersonian newspaper editors who criticized Adams. The unpopularity of these laws led to the defeat of President Adams in the election of 1800 and to the election of Thomas Jefferson, whose administration repealed these acts.

The primary author of the Declaration of Independence, Thomas Jefferson was the first president to be inaugurated in the new capital of Washington, D.C. His election was just the first of a string of victories for the Democratic-Republican party. The Federalist Party shrank, and then disappeared. Long interested in the Western territories for the United States, Jefferson sponsored the Lewis and Clark expedition, in which Meriwether Lewis and William Clark explored and mapped much of the territory extending to the Pacific Ocean. The fear of getting involved in the wars then raging between France and England prompted Jefferson to buy the territory of Louisiana from France in 1803. This transaction, known as the Louisiana Purchase, removed France from the land on America's borders, and it joined to the United States the city of New Orleans, the entire Mississippi River valley,

A colored map of United States territories shows the Louisiana Purchase. President Thomas Jefferson bought the land from France in 1803.

and what we now call the American Midwest. This acquisition doubled the size of the United States.

The fourth president, James Madison, was another Founding Father. In the same way that Jefferson was the primary author of the Declaration of Independence, Madison was the principal author of the Constitution. The biggest event of Madison's two terms as president was the War of 1812. Ignoring George Washington's warning about European conflicts, the United States joined France in its war against England. When the English defeated the French in Europe, British troops turned on France's partner, the United States.

The early part of the war saw the British invade Washington, D.C., and set fire to the **White House** and the domed Capitol, the building that houses Congress. In fact, British soldiers freely roamed the nation's capital. Admiral Cockburn, the British commander, even gathered his

troops in the House of Representatives. "'Gentlemen,' he said, 'the question is, Shall this harbor of Yankee democracy be burned? All in favor of burning it will say aye!' The vote in favor was unanimous. 'Light up,' said Cockburn," and the building was set afire.

The White House was abandoned when British troops burned Washington, D.C. in 1814. First Lady Dolley Madison insisted that Gilbert Stuart's large portrait of George Washington be removed and taken to safety.

American soldiers, however, eventually began to defeat the British in naval and land battles. In the Battle of New Orleans, U.S. troops, led by General Andrew Jackson, killed about half of the attacking British force of 5,000 soldiers while suffering very few casualties.

The United States gained Florida from Spain under the next president, James Monroe, who became most famous for the Monroe Doctrine, which stated that North and South America were at that time closed to European nations seeking control of these lands. Sounding much like George Washington, who warned Americans not to become too involved with other nations, Monroe told the Europeans that, in return for their promise not to become involved in the Americas, the United States would not interfere with the nations of Europe.

The other major event of Monroe's presidency was the acceptance by Congress of the Missouri Compromise, the first major attempt to satisfy both the slave states of the South and the antislavery states of the North. During this period, the states north of Maryland and Delaware had abolished slavery, but slavery continued in the South, and the conflict over it began to spread. There were two reasons why Americans began to argue over slavery. The first was the role of the abolitionists, antislavery activists who emerged in the North. Not satisfied with eliminating slavery in their own states, the abolitionists got their name because they wanted to abolish slavery in all states, including the South.

The second source of this growing conflict was disagreement over whether slavery should be expanded into the new U.S. territories in the West. Southern pioneers took their slaves with them; Northerners moving to the West continued to oppose slavery. As each new territory or state joined the United States, some people wanted slavery to be legal in the new lands; others argued against it. This was the problem the Missouri Compromise resolved, but only for a time. Originally part of the Louisiana Purchase, Missouri wanted to join the United States as a slave state. This, however, would have upset the balance between slave states and antislave states, which were equal in number. To allow Missouri to become a slave state while maintaining antislave/slave balance among all states, antislavery Maine was also made a state. In addition, the compromise stated that slavery was not allowed in the rest of the Louisiana Purchase territory north of the southern boundary of Missouri. In this way, the dividing line between the North and South was extended across the Western territories.

The period during which the Founding Fathers served as America's first presidents began coming to an end when Thomas Jefferson of Virginia and John Adams of

Massachusetts, the Founding Fathers who had signed the Declaration of Independence and who had both later served as president, died on the same day. The date was July 4, 1826, exactly 50 years after they declared America's independence.

Two years later, the era of the Founding Fathers finally came to an end when John Quincy Adams, the son of John Adams—and the only child of a president to become president so far—lost reelection to a second term. The winner of the 1828 election was Andrew Jackson, the hero of the Battle of New Orleans, who would forever change the presidency.

A painting of the signing of the Declaration of Independence by John Trumbull. John Adams is the first standing figure on the left; Thomas Jefferson stands second from right.

CHAPTER 3

Democracy, Slavery, Expansion, and Civil War:
From Andrew Jackson to Andrew Johnson

BORN TO A POOR family and orphaned at 14, Andrew Jackson was popular among average Americans, who saw him as "one of them." The Battle of New Orleans made him the best-known hero of his time. By the time of Jackson's election, Americans were no longer required to own property in order to vote, which meant that poor white males could vote for the first time. All of these developments made Jackson's two terms as president seem like a movement toward more equality and opportunity in America. Some call this time the period of the "common man." Jackson's election also represented the birth of the Democratic Party—the new name for Jefferson's old Democratic-Republicans—which is still with us today.

To reward his supporters, Jackson started the *spoils system,* in which the people who voted for him were rewarded with jobs (or "spoils") in his government. Jackson stopped meeting with his cabinet and instead sought advice from a group of friends and supporters, who became famous as the Kitchen Cabinet. Jackson engaged in a long feud with the Bank of the United States, which he felt was run by rich and powerful men who did not care about Jackson's supporters.

It was during the Jackson administration that former President John Quincy Adams was elected to Congress in 1830, the only president—so far—to serve in Congress after serving as president. Adams was an outspoken opponent of slavery during the 17 years he served in Congress. He collapsed and died on the floor of the House of Representatives at the age of 80.

At the end of his second term, President Jackson was powerful enough to help his vice president, Martin Van Buren, win the 1836 presidential election. Jackson's opponents, however, created a new political party that year, the Whig party, whose candidate for president, William Henry Harrison, defeated Van Buren in 1840.

President Harrison delivered the longest inaugural address but had the shortest presidency of all. He caught pneumonia during his 1841 inauguration and died 31 days later. Harrison was the first of eight presidents to die in office. His death focused attention on the unclear wording of the Constitution regarding how or whether a vice president takes the place of a president who has died. For Harrison's vice president, John Tyler—who was on his knees playing marbles when he learned that Harrison had died—the issue was resolved when Congress voted to recognize him as president. Death and illness among presidents would continue to cause trouble.

During his single term, President Tyler's most important act was to sign the congressional resolution of 1845 that made a state of Texas, whose settlers had fought off the Mexican army and declared Texas independent in 1836. The annexation of Texas led to war with Mexico, which began under the man who followed Tyler into the

White House, President James K. Polk. U.S. soldiers led by General Zachary Taylor defeated Mexico, whose troops retreated south of the Rio Grande, the river that is the current border with Mexico. This event gave the United States the state of California and the region now known as the American Southwest.

Like Andrew Jackson, General Taylor rode his wartime victory to the White House, but Taylor almost missed his chance. When the Whig party nominated Taylor, the letter officially notifying him of his nomination carried no postage. Back then, postage was paid not by stamps applied by the sender but by the person who received the mail. As a war hero, Taylor received stacks of letters from all over the country but usually refused to accept them because of the cost.

Eventually, Taylor received word of his nomination and won the election of 1848. He served only 16 months in office when he became ill and died.

When Vice President Millard Fillmore became president, he tried to steer a middle course between the proslavery

A map of the United States showing territorial shifts and acquisitions from 1783 to 1845. Texas (highlighted in blue at bottom center), a former Mexican territory, was declared a state in 1845.

and antislavery elements within his Whig Party, but the party rejected him. The Whigs—the party of Presidents Harrison, Tyler, Taylor, and Fillmore—split apart over slavery and disappeared. Another one-term president, Franklin Pierce, who also failed to bridge the differences between the North and the South, followed Fillmore. But it was during Pierce's presidency that the antislavery forces founded the Republican Party in 1854.

Like so many presidents before him, Democrat James Buchanan tried—and failed—to please both sides of the growing conflict over slavery; like his predecessors, he served only one term. This conflict, it was becoming clear, could not be resolved by normal political compromise. Tensions were building. In 1860, finally, the election of Abraham Lincoln, the candidate of the antislavery Republican Party, lit the fuse that exploded into the American Civil War.

Month by month, events led quickly to war. Lincoln was elected in November 1860, and South Carolina seceded (withdrew from) the United States in December. Six other Southern states followed South Carolina and, by February, they had created an entirely new nation, the Confederacy. The Confederacy had its own president, Jefferson Davis, a former Democratic U.S. senator from Mississippi.

President Lincoln was at first prepared to let slavery continue in the South, though he opposed its extension into the new territories. In his March 1861 inaugural address, however, Lincoln warned that he would "preserve, protect, and defend" the United States or "the Union." Lincoln told the South, "With you, and not with me, is the solemn question of 'Shall it be peace, or a sword?'" South Carolina responded in April by attacking Fort Sumter, a Union military base in Charleston that Lincoln had refused to close. Lincoln's call for troops to respond prompted four more states to join the Confederacy, for a total of 11.

Quickly organized but largely unprepared, the Union army marched south from Washington, D.C., to capture

the southern capital, Richmond, Virginia. The Confederate army, however, met and defeated the Union troops at the Battle of Bull Run (also called the Battle of Manassas), the first of many victories of the Confederate army, most of them under the leadership of General Robert E. Lee.

Eager to defeat the South and end the war, Lincoln could not at first find a general who would aggressively attack the Confederate army and win. To one early commander of the Union army, General George McClellan, Lincoln wrote, "My dear McClellan: If you don't want to use the army, I should like to borrow it for a while. Yours respectfully, A. Lincoln." There were, however, more men and material resources in the North than in the South, and in Ulysses S. Grant, Lincoln eventually found a general who would not only fight, but win.

After the Union victory in the Battle of Antietam, President Lincoln in 1863 issued his famous Emancipation Proclamation, which freed all slaves within the Confederate states. This proclamation transformed a war to preserve the Union into a more popular fight for freedom. Later that

South Carolina's bombardment of Fort Sumter on April 18, 1861, answered the question President Lincoln posed in his inaugural address, "Shall it be peace, or a sword?"

Atlanta, Georgia's, streets overflow with wounded Confederate soldiers in this scene from the MGM film Gone With the Wind. *The fall of Atlanta signaled the collapse of the Confederacy.*

same year, following the Union's victory at Gettysburg, Pennsylvania, Lincoln delivered perhaps his most famous speech, the Gettysburg Address, in which he asked Americans to dedicate themselves once again to "the proposition that all men are created equal."

Finally, in 1865, four years after South Carolina fired on Fort Sumter, General Lee surrendered his shrunken and tattered army to General Grant.

Almost 500,000 soldiers had been killed on both sides, more than 280,000 were wounded, and much of the South lay in ruins. The war had opened painful divisions between friends, and even families. For example, at the meeting where General Grant accepted General Lee's surrender, Grant recognized several of Lee's military assistants—close friends who had been members of Grant's wedding party. General McClellan, whom President Lincoln had placed in charge of the Union army, tried to unseat Lincoln in the 1864 presidential election. Lincoln won a second term, but the deaths and divisions of war would not be soon forgotten.

Five days after General Lee surrendered, an actor who had favored the Confederacy, John Wilkes Booth, shot Lin-

coln as the president watched a play at Ford's Theater in Washington. Lincoln died the next day, becoming the first president to be assassinated. Lincoln would be remembered as one of America's greatest presidents, yet the nation's wounds, like Lincoln's, would not heal.

Men of the 107th United States Colored Infantry pose for Mathew Brady in wartime.

Disagreements over how to treat the southern states after the war, during the period called Reconstruction, led Lincoln's vice president and successor, Andrew Johnson, to become the first president to be impeached by the House and put on trial by the Senate. A native of Tennessee, who was accused by Northerners of being too easy on the defeated South, Johnson was found not guilty by one vote. Before he completed Lincoln's second term and left office, Johnson approved America's purchase of Alaska from Russia.

The driving of a "Golden Spike" symbolized the completion of the first United States transcontinental railroad in 1869. Railroads contributed to a period of massive industrial growth.

CHAPTER 4

Industrialization, Reform, and the World:
Ulysses Grant to William McKinley

LIKE PRESIDENTS Washington, Jackson, and Taylor, Ulysses Grant was elected in 1868 based on his wartime popularity as a military commander. Made a full general after the war, Grant was the first citizen since Washington to hold that rank. But American society had begun to change before and during the war, and Grant was largely unprepared to lead a dramatically changing nation.

New and ever larger factories were being built. Aided by railroads and telegraph lines that were crisscrossing the country, huge oil and steel industries emerged. New products were being invented. People left their farms for the growing cities of New York, Chicago, and Philadelphia, where they were joined by waves of immigrants from Europe. Factory workers began to complain about the demands placed on them and about dangerous working conditions. They began to organize labor unions and to seek the help of government. Government was also urged to do something about the growing numbers of poor people in the cities.

Whereas many Americans were becoming wealthier, Americans who owned factories or led large industries became very wealthy, indeed. Like the workers, these rich industrialists sought to influence the government. In fact, attempts to illegally influence the government—by secretly paying government officials, for instance—led to many scandals, which marked Grant's two terms as president.

These developments also encouraged presidents to expand their power over business and employment. The growth of big cities, large industries, and huge financial fortunes, moreover, was making America a wealthy and powerful nation, one that would begin to send its armies around the world. As America became more powerful, so would American presidents.

Workers in the Pittsburgh, Pennsylvania, Steel Works around 1905. Factory workers had begun seeking the government's help with their working conditions and forming labor unions.

Grant's successor, Rutherford B. Hayes, was appointed president by the Congress after the election of 1876, in which some southern states submitted two different sets of votes. Hayes thought he had lost the election to Democrat Samuel Tilden, but a committee appointed by Congress awarded all of the disputed votes to Hayes. Keeping a promise to Southerners, Hayes removed the last soldiers who had occupied the South since the Civil War, thereby ending Reconstruction. Having angered his fellow Republicans, Hayes did not seek a second term.

Yet another Republican followed Hayes into the White House, but not for long. James A. Garfield was president only a few months when, in 1881, a man who had supported him—but who was unhappy that he did not receive a government job in return—shot the president at a railroad station in Washington, D.C. Garfield died two months later, and his death prompted Congress to approve the Civil Service Act of 1883 or Pendleton Act. Reversing the spoils system President Andrew Jackson made popular, the Civil Service Act required that government employees be hired for their skills rather than for the level of political support they give to a president.

Keeping secret the news that he had a fatal illness, Vice President Chester A. Arthur became president and completed Garfield's term in office.

The Republicans lost their first presidential election since Lincoln's when Democrat Grover Cleveland was elected in 1884. This was not the only reason Republicans should have feared Cleveland, for he was an executioner. Indeed, as a sheriff in New York State, Cleveland had personally hung many convicted criminals. In 1886, during Cleveland's first term, the Statue of Liberty, a gift from France, was dedicated.

Cleveland was defeated for reelection by Benjamin Harrison. Perhaps Harrison's most important move was to sign the Sherman Anti-Trust Act of 1890, which attempted to break up the large industries that had eliminated their competitors or had tried to place limits on competition.

After four years, Cleveland returned to fight again in 1892 and defeated Harrison's attempt to win reelection. This made Cleveland the only president to serve two, nonconsecutive terms. As a result, Cleveland is considered the 22nd as well as the 24th president. In his second term Cleveland became the first president to use the army to break up a labor strike. Strikes were a new but increasingly common tactic of workers, who would refuse to work until their wages or working conditions were improved. Cleveland's use of the army ended a major strike by railroad workers, which had brought the transportation of people, freight, and even mail to a halt in most of the nation in 1894.

Throughout this period, Americans had come to sympathize with the residents of the island of Cuba, who were fighting rulers from Spain. Like most Americans, however, William McKinley, who had been elected president in 1896, hoped to avoid a war with Spain over Cuba. Then, in 1898, the U.S. battleship *Maine* exploded and sank in a Cuban harbor, killing 260 men. Though it was not proved that Spain sank the *Maine*, the American people were getting even more angry at Spain.

During this period, it was said that newspaper publisher William Randolph Hearst hoped the conflict with Spain would help sell more of his newspapers. Some people believed Hearst reported events in such a way as to make a war even more likely. For instance, Hearst sent a famous American painter, Frederic Remington, to Cuba to get dramatic illustrations of Cubans fighting the Spanish. Nothing was happening when Remington arrived. "There is no trouble here," he wrote to Hearst. "There will be no war. I wish to return." Hearst wrote back, "Please remain. You furnish the pictures and I'll furnish the war."

McKinley asked Congress for permission to intervene in Cuba, and Congress said yes. Spain replied by declaring war on the United States. The Spanish-American War had begun. American naval forces quickly destroyed Spanish warships in Cuban waters as well as in the Philippine Islands, a Spanish territory in the South Pacific Ocean. Meanwhile, about 17,000 U.S. soldiers—including a future president, Theodore (Teddy) Roosevelt—defeated the Spanish troops in Cuba. The war was over in a few months, and less than 2,500 American soldiers had died.

The United States battleship Maine *explodes in the harbor of Havana, Cuba, in 1898. Many Americans believed that Spain was responsible.*

As a result of the war, America gained control of Cuba, as well as the Spanish possessions of Puerto Rico, which is an island neighbor of Cuba's, the island of Guam in the Pacific Ocean, and the Philippine Islands. Also in 1898, for reasons unrelated to the war, the United States annexed the islands of Hawaii. For the first time, America had become a major naval power and a world power.

*United States troops
in the Battle of San
Juan Hill, Cuba,
July 1–2, 1898.*

President McKinley was reelected in 1900 with a new vice president, Teddy Roosevelt. As a leader of the Rough Riders, a group of cowboys-turned-soldiers who participated in the famous Battle of San Juan Hill in the Spanish-American War, Roosevelt was elected governor of New York on the basis of his wartime fame. But corrupt Republicans who could not control the young Roosevelt turned against him. In an attempt to get him out of New York, they pushed

Theodore Roosevelt led the Rough Riders during the Spanish-American War in 1898.

him in the direction of McKinley and the White House. This might have been the end of Roosevelt's career, since few vice presidents became president during this period. That all changed, however, when McKinley was shot and killed by a lone gunman in 1901 at an exhibition in Buffalo, New York.

At the age of 42, Teddy Roosevelt became America's youngest president. Like Andrew Jackson before him, he would forever change the presidency.

A vessel traveling south through the Gatun Locks of the Panama Canal. The new South American nation of Panama was created in 1903 to accommodate the canal.

CHAPTER **5**

Reform, World War, and the Depression:
Theodore Roosevelt to Herbert Hoover

AN ENERGETIC AND ADVENTUROUS MAN, Teddy Roosevelt did not believe presidents should be limited to the role described for them in the Constitution or laid out for them by tradition. Instead, Roosevelt used all of his skills and energy to accomplish everything he thought was right. He expanded government power at home and abroad, and he made the presidency more powerful.

Prompted by journalists and others who had exposed bad business practices, Roosevelt insisted that the government has a right to control (or regulate) business—for example, by inspecting meat plants and enforcing safety rules for drugs. He used the Sherman Anti-Trust Act to break up large industries that attempted to limit competition from other businesses. An avid hunter, explorer, and outdoorsman, he placed millions of acres of land under government control to conserve some of America's natural resources from the mining and timber industries.

Roosevelt was just as active in extending U.S. power overseas, where, he said, America should "speak softly and carry a big stick."

President Roosevelt created an entirely new nation in South America, for instance, in order to build the Panama Canal, which would connect the Atlantic and Pacific Oceans and increase waterborne trade. When the South American country of Colombia refused to approve a treaty allowing the United States to build the canal in Colombia's Panama region, canal supporters and local residents rebelled and declared Panama an independent country in 1903. U.S. Navy warships prevented Colombia from defeating the rebels, and America quickly recognized the new nation. (After a construction period of seven years, the Panama Canal was formally opened in 1915, under American control.) Roosevelt ran for election in his own right in 1904 and won easily. After helping to end a war between Russia and Japan, Roosevelt was awarded the 1906 Nobel Peace Prize.

In 1908 Roosevelt helped William H. Taft, a close friend who had served in his administration, gain the Republican nomination for president. The heaviest man ever to serve as president, Taft weighed 350 pounds.

Perhaps the two most important things President Taft did were to ask the states for their approval on two proposals: (1) to enact a tax on personal income and (2) to require U.S. senators to be elected directly by the voters rather than being appointed by state legislatures. Both measures were approved by the states in 1913 as amendments to the U.S. Constitution.

Though Taft continued many of Roosevelt's policies, the former president considered Taft too conservative. As a result, in 1912, even though Taft had Republican support to run for a second term, Roosevelt opposed him with his own Progressive Party (also called the Bull Moose Party). By splitting the Republican Party, Roosevelt almost guaranteed that the Democratic presidential candidate, Woodrow Wilson, would win the election—and he did.

A campaign button for Theodore Roosevelt's Bull Moose Party, 1912.

Just as John Quincy Adams returned to government service after his presidency by serving in Congress, former President Taft later served as chief justice—the top judge on the Supreme Court—from 1921 to 1930.

The first Southerner elected president since the Civil War, Woodrow Wilson built on the government reforms of his predecessors, such as limiting the demands employers could place on workers and forcing business to conduct free and fair trade. He revived the practice, abandoned by Thomas Jefferson in 1801, of addressing Congress in person. Four amendments to the Constitution were approved by the states under President Wilson. These amendments introduced the personal income tax, required U.S. senators to be elected directly by the voters rather than be appointed by state legislatures, made alcoholic drinks illegal, and gave women the right to vote.

The biggest event of Wilson's presidency, however, was the outbreak of World War I in Europe in August 1914, when Germany and Austria-Hungary went to war against Russia, France, and Great Britain, plunging much of the world into the deadliest conflict ever known.

Wilson tried to keep America out of the war by keeping the United States neutral, or uninvolved. German submarines, however, fired on and sank ships traveling

Twenty-eighth president Woodrow Wilson built on the government reforms of his predecessors.

between the United States and Europe, killing hundreds and angering the American people. President Wilson was reelected in 1916 on the basis of the slogan, "He kept us out of war." Wilson tried but failed to bring an end to the war. Then Germany began sinking American ships once again. In 1917 Wilson asked for and received from Congress a declaration of war against Germany. The war would give President Wilson more power to regulate business and personal freedoms.

American soldiers—more than 116,000 of whom would die—tipped the balance of fighting in favor of the British, French, and Russian forces, thus defeating Germany. Austria-Hungry split into many smaller countries, and Russia experienced a revolution, bringing to power a Communist regime, which changed the name of the nation to the Soviet Union. President Wilson was very active in negotiating an end to the war. Like Teddy Roosevelt, Wilson was awarded the Nobel Peace Prize. Wilson's plan to have all of the countries of the world join the League of Nations, an organization that would work to avoid another major war, suffered a defeat when the U.S. Senate refused to let America join the new organization.

Wilson was traveling around the country, trying to win popular support for the League of Nations when, in the fall of 1919, he suffered a serious stroke, an illness affecting the brain and central nervous system. At first, the president was totally disabled and unable to work. After two months he recovered slightly but was still physically and mentally impaired. The seriousness of the president's illness was largely kept a secret. Wilson grew a long beard and saw only his wife, doctor, and secretary. He served the rest of his second term in isolation and defeat.

The election of 1920—the first in which women could vote—saw a return to the Republican Party and the election of Warren G. Harding, who had appealed for a "return to normalcy." It was President Harding who appointed former President Taft to the Supreme Court. Harding's presidency was overshadowed by a scandal involving two

American soldiers like these, shown firing into enemy lines, helped bring about the defeat of Germany and Austria-Hungary in World War I.

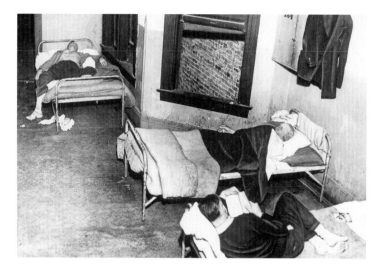

The people shown in this Los Angeles "flophouse" (cheap rooming house or hotel) may have lost their homes or jobs in the Great Depression of the 1930s.

members of his cabinet, one of whom—Secretary of the Interior Albert Fall—was convicted and imprisoned for accepting bribes. Returning from a trip to Alaska in 1923, President Harding became ill and died in San Francisco. Vice President Calvin Coolidge succeeded Harding as president.

Known as "Silent Cal," President Coolidge would sit through social occasions without uttering a syllable. The story is told that a woman dinner companion told the president she had made a bet with her friends that she could get him to say more than three words. "You lose," Coolidge replied. President Coolidge won election in his own right in 1924 but did not seek a second term of his own in 1928.

Coolidge was followed by Herbert Hoover, who entered the White House with a worldwide reputation as a great administrator but left office with perhaps the worst reputation among all presidents because of an event, the Great Depression, that was largely beyond the power of any leader.

Throughout the 1920s, the U.S. economy grew rapidly, and there were reasons to believe prosperity would continue forever. After all, the winner of the 1928 election, Herbert Hoover, had won international acclaim as the man who channeled food, clothes, and other support to the millions of refugees in Europe during and after World War I.

President Franklin D. Roosevelt speaking directly to the American people in one of his "fireside chats." Roosevelt explained the government's efforts to bring about economic recovery.

He had also served as secretary of commerce under Presidents Harding and Coolidge. A thoroughly modern executive, Hoover was the first president to have a telephone on his desk.

Yet within months of Hoover's taking office in 1929, the U.S. economy suddenly collapsed, pushing millions of people out of work, closing scores of businesses, even wiping out the fortunes of many wealthy Americans. Thrown out of their homes because they were unable to pay for them, many Americans lived in primitive, homemade camps they called Hoovervilles. The confidence of the entire nation was shattered. Hoover tried without success to turn the economy around, a task made harder because the depression was worldwide. Even more fatal to his popularity, Hoover opposed most plans to provide federal aid to the growing masses of unemployed, desperate Americans.

In the election of 1932, it surprised no one that Democrat Franklin D. Roosevelt defeated Hoover. But most Americans at that time could not have guessed that Roosevelt would become our longest-serving president, that he would remake the presidency in his various attempts to bring an end to the Great Depression, and that he would achieve victory in yet another world war.

Hoover Dam, built largely by unemployed workers under President Roosevelt's WPA (Work Projects Administration) program.

CHAPTER **6**

The New Deal, World War, and the Cold War:
Franklin Roosevelt to William J. Clinton

THE LAST PRESIDENT to be inaugurated on the fourth of March after an election year (the 20th Amendment to the Constitution moved the date up to January 20), Roosevelt took office by telling Americans that "the only thing we have to fear is fear itself."

Although he had pledged "a new deal" for the American people, Roosevelt did not have a plan to eliminate the depression. He had spent his whole life preparing for the presidency, following the same path to the White House laid down by his cousin, Teddy Roosevelt. Like Teddy, Franklin had served as a state legislator, assistant secretary of the Navy, and governor of New York.

Overwhelmed by the economic crisis of the Great Depression, Congress surrendered a great deal of power to Roosevelt, whose administration enacted dozens of emergency measures, such as closing the banks. Major new laws were passed to regulate business, and the government began borrowing and spending money in the hopes that paying the unemployed to build dams and bridges, for instance, would spark an economic recovery. In so-called "fireside chats," Roosevelt explained his actions to the American people in speeches on the radio. Under Roosevelt, the 21st Amendment took effect, making alcoholic drinks legal for the first time since 1919.

These efforts were enough to win reelection for Roosevelt in 1936, but the economy continued to falter. In addition, critics complained that Roosevelt was acquiring too much power. When the Supreme Court ruled against some of his laws because they violated the Constitution, for instance, Roosevelt tried to "pack" the nine-member Supreme Court with more judges—ones who would approve his plans. This sparked a firestorm of criticism, and Roosevelt changed his mind.

Overseas, meanwhile, Japan was waging war in East Asia, while Germany's Nazi regime, led by Adolf Hitler, was conquering Europe. Indeed, the election of 1940 took place in the looming shadow of war. In this environment, Roosevelt broke with tradition and sought a third term, the first president to do so. Roosevelt was bitterly criticized but won reelection nonetheless.

A little more than a year later, on December 7, 1941, the Japanese bombed the U.S. naval base at Pearl Harbor, Hawaii, plunging America into World War II. Because Japan, Germany, and Italy were allies, the United States was at war all over the world. The production of war materials revived the economy and, by 1944, victory looked probable. As a result, Roosevelt, despite failing health, was elected to a fourth term. In April, 1945, three months into his new term, Roosevelt died, ending the longest tenure of any U.S. president.

"Last night the moon, the stars and all the planets fell on me," Vice President Harry S. Truman, as the new president, told reporters the next day. "If you fellows ever pray, pray for me." A modest, plain-speaking man, Truman seemed unprepared for the presidency. Yet he quickly made

many life-and-death decisions that helped end the war and protect the United States and its allies from a new threat—the Soviet Union.

The battleship USS Maryland *sinks during the Japanese attack on Pearl Harbor, December 7, 1941.*

More than 400,000 U.S. soldiers would die before the armies of the United States and Soviet Russia defeated and occupied Germany in 1945. Germany formally surrendered a month after Roosevelt died, but Japan fought on, and many more American lives would be lost if Japan were to be invaded. Upon becoming president, Truman was told that an entirely new kind of weapon—a nuclear bomb—had been developed in secret, and it was ready to be used. Therefore, President Truman decided to drop these nuclear bombs on two Japanese cities. They created such unparalleled devastation—completely destroying both cities—that Japan quickly surrendered, saving the lives of perhaps tens of thousands of American soldiers.

The war was over, yet world conflict and attempts to end it would dominate Truman's presidency. President Truman quickly created several international organizations to protect America and its allies. Reversing its earlier rejection of the League of Nations, for instance, America led the effort to create a new international organization to deter war, called the United Nations. But the United Nations could do nothing when the Soviet Union refused to leave the area they occupied during the war. This left the nations of Eastern Europe, including the eastern half of Germany, under Soviet rule and without freedom.

Following his come-from-behind election victory in 1948, President Truman faced even greater threats, such as the Soviet acquisition of nuclear bombs and a Communist takeover of China. In response, Truman created the North Atlantic Treaty Organization (NATO), which organized the Western European nations (including Western Germany) for defense against the Soviet Union. The U.S.–Soviet confrontation spread throughout the world and came to be known as the Cold War. Communist North Korea invaded South Korea in 1950, but with the backing of the United Nations, President Truman waged a war to free South Korea. This was achieved by 1953 but at the loss of more than 54,000 U.S. soldiers.

Aided by charges that Communists held positions in Truman's administration, Republicans won the presidential election of 1952 with a war hero, Dwight D. Eisenhower, who commanded the American and Allied armies in Europe during World War II. Following a depression and two wars, President Eisenhower's two terms are remembered for their peace and prosperity. He started America's network of highways, and he sent soldiers to Little Rock, Arkansas, to force all-white schools to accept African-American students. Following a heart attack, Eisenhower became the first president whose health was discussed publicly.

Democrats retook the White House in the election of 1960 with the handsome and wealthy U.S. Senator John F. Kennedy. In defeating Eisenhower's vice president, Richard M. Nixon, Kennedy, 43, became America's youngest *elected* president. (Teddy Roosevelt was 42 when he became president, but he was not *elected* to his first term.) Kennedy was also the first Roman Catholic president.

Cold War tensions marked President Kennedy's presidency. These included the Cuban Missile Crisis (see Chapter 1) and the building of the Berlin Wall by the Soviet Union, a barricade that prevented East Germans from escaping to the West. Kennedy promised to put Americans on the moon within 10 years and sent larger numbers of military advisors to South Vietnam, a nation in Southeast Asia that was being threatened by Communist North Vietnam. His presidency was cut short, however, when an assassin shot and killed the president while he traveled in a motorcade through Dallas, Texas, in 1963.

Kennedy's vice president, Lyndon B. Johnson, tried to defend South Vietnam with increasing numbers of soldiers, and the Vietnam War intensified. He also tried to wage a war against poverty at home by increasing aid to the poor. In 1964, a year after Kennedy's assassination, Johnson was overwhelmingly elected on his own. Yet Americans increasingly came into conflict with one another. College students demonstrated against the war and African Americans, led by Martin Luther King Jr., protested their unequal treatment. Protesting students were shot and killed

The 1968 Poor People's March on Washington, D.C., commemorated children killed in a 1963 church bombing in Birmingham, Alabama. Protest arose from many levels of American society during this era.

by soldiers on a college campus in Ohio, and King was assassinated.

Weary of these conflicts, Johnson did not seek reelection. Instead, former Vice President Richard Nixon was elected president in 1968, promising to end the Vietnam War and restore order to American society. Skilled in dealing with other nations, Republican President Nixon made progress in withdrawing U.S. soldiers from Vietnam, and he developed better relations with the Soviet Union and China. He also fulfilled a promise of the late President Kennedy—Americans landed on the moon in 1969. Nixon was reelected in 1972, but his administration was soon overtaken by scandals.

Nixon's vice president, Spiro Agnew, resigned in a bribery scandal and was replaced by Congressman Gerald Ford. Then, investigations of a White House–linked burglary of Democratic party offices at the Watergate Hotel in Washington involved Nixon in the Watergate scandal. In 1974, shortly after a committee of the House of Representatives recommended that he be impeached, Nixon resigned.

Not only was Nixon the first president to resign, but Vice President Ford became our first president to serve without being elected to either the presidency or the vice presidency. Ford oversaw the final withdrawal of American soldiers from Vietnam, but a slowdown of the economy and growing inflation (a decline in the value of money) marked his presidency. Still, analysts believe Ford could have won the 1976 election if he had not pardoned former President Nixon for "all crimes he may have committed while in office."

Instead, the victor was Democrat Jimmy Carter. President Carter negotiated a peace agreement between Israel and Egypt and he negotiated a treaty returning the Panama Canal to Panama. His presidency, however, was marked by more inflation and gasoline shortages. Overseas, Soviet-backed forces took power in several nations, and the Soviet Union invaded Afghanistan in 1979. America, by contrast, appeared weak when revolutionaries captured the U.S. Embassy in Iran and took 52 Americans hostage. A rescue attempt failed.

These troubles led Americans to reject President Carter for Republican Ronald Reagan in 1980. After surviving an assassination attempt two months into his term, President Reagan began making major changes: reducing regulations on business, cutting taxes, and increasing defense spending. His inability to reduce other government spending pushed the government into debt, and the economy slowed sharply in his first term. Reagan regained popularity after the United States overthrew a violent Communist regime on the Caribbean island of Grenada in 1983. The economy also began to strengthen. When Reagan was reelected in 1984, he was, at 73, the oldest man ever to win the office.

In President Reagan's second term, his administration's aggressive challenges to Soviet power worldwide—by placing missiles in Western Europe, for instance, and supporting anti-Soviet rebels in Afghanistan and Nicaragua—pushed the Soviet Union to try to improve its internal weaknesses. As the Soviet Union tried to make its society freer, it began to crumble.

President Reagan's popularity helped his vice president, George Bush, win the presidency in 1988. Under Bush, the Soviet Union gave up Communism, embraced freedom, and broke up into many smaller nations, including Russia. Meanwhile, Iraq invaded Kuwait in 1990. President Bush assembled armies from many nations and expelled Iraq from Kuwait. After breaking a promise not to raise taxes and being unable to stop an economic slowdown, Bush was defeated for reelection by Democrat William J. Clinton.

President Clinton tried, but failed, to reform America's health-care system in his first term. Following the Republican takeover of Congress in 1994—for the first time since 1952—the president adopted many Republican

Hillary Rodham Clinton's run for the United States Senate made her the first First Lady to seek elective office. As the American presidency continues to become more powerful, other changes may lie ahead.

proposals, such as reforming aid programs for the poor, which were approved by Congress. Yet Clinton was soon embroiled in scandal, which led to impeachment charges that accused him of lying to a jury. While the House voted to impeach him, just as with President Andrew Johnson, the Senate did not convict him. In President Clinton's second term, **First Lady** Hillary Rodham Clinton ran for election to the U.S. Senate, the first First Lady to seek elective office from the White House.

The Founding Fathers would probably be shocked at how powerful U.S. presidents have become. But they could not have predicted how large, wealthy, and powerful a nation the United States of America would become. Nor could they have predicted the large-scale crises and world

wars that Americans have survived through the aid of an empowered presidency. Wars and other crises, then, not only made the office much more powerful and demanded more of our presidents, but these events continue to determine how important presidents are and how much power they have.

Allied troops assembled by President Bush for "Operation Desert Storm" in the 1991 Persian Gulf War.

The Presidents and Their Terms of Service

(Boldface designates presidents who died in office.)

George Washington (1789–1797)

John Adams (1797–1801)

Thomas Jefferson (1801–1809)

James Madison (1809–1817)

James Monroe (1817–1825)

John Quincy Adams (1825–1829)

Andrew Jackson (1829–1837)

Martin Van Buren (1837–1841)

William H. Harrison (1841)

John Tyler (1841–1845)

James K. Polk (1845–1849)

Zachary Taylor (1849–1850)

Millard Fillmore (1850–1853)

Franklin Pierce (1853–1857)

James Buchanan (1857–1861)

Abraham Lincoln (1861–1865)

Andrew Johnson (1865–1869)

Ulysses S. Grant (1869–1877)

Rutherford B. Hayes (1877–1881)

James A. Garfield (1881)

Chester A. Arthur (1881–1885)

Grover Cleveland (1885–1889)

Benjamin Harrison (1889–1893)

Grover Cleveland (1893–1897)

William McKinley (1897–1901)

Theodore Roosevelt (1901–1909)

William Howard Taft (1909–1913)

Woodrow Wilson (1913–1921)

Warren G. Harding (1921–1923)

Calvin Coolidge (1923–1929)

Herbert Hoover (1929–1933)

Franklin D. Roosevelt (1933–1945)

Harry S. Truman (1945–1953)

Dwight D. Eisenhower (1953–1961)

John F. Kennedy (1961–1963)

Lyndon B. Johnson (1963–1969)

Richard M. Nixon (1969–1974)

Gerald Ford (1974–1977)

James (Jimmy) Carter (1977–1981)

Ronald Reagan (1981–1989)

George Bush (1989–1993)

William J. Clinton (1993–2001)

Glossary

Cabinet—The leaders of the largest or most important departments of the executive branch of government, such as the attorney general, who manages the Department of Justice, and secretary of state, who is in charge of the State Department.

Camp David—A private, wooded resort in Maryland for use by presidents who want to get away from the White House, where they both live and work. President Dwight D. Eisenhower gave the facility its current name, in honor of his grandson.

Constitution—The document that created the original government of the United States, including the presidency, and established America's most important laws.

First Lady—The informal title of the wife of the president. The first recorded use of the term was in 1863 by a British newspaper reporter, who referred to Mary Todd Lincoln as "the first Lady in the Land."

Impeachment—The only method allowed by the Constitution for removing a president from office. Impeachment is similar to a trial, but conducted by Congress. Only the House of Representatives can bring charges (by majority vote); the Senate requires a two-thirds vote to convict and remove a president.

Inauguration—The formal ceremony during which the president takes the oath of office, which officially makes him president. The ceremony includes an inaugural address, which is the first major speech a president makes. Originally held March 4 following a November presidential election, the 20th Amendment moved the date up to January 20. Presidents are still elected in even-numbered years, and they take the oath of office in the following, odd-numbered years.

Separation of powers—The method used by the Founding Fathers to make sure the U.S. government did not have a concentrated power that could be used against the will of the people, such as the power wielded by kings or dictators. The authors of the Constitution identified three major powers of government—legislative, executive, and judicial—and gave those powers to three separate branches of government—the Congress, the presidency, and the judiciary.

State of the Union message—An annual report by the president to the Congress. This is a requirement of the Constitution. It says presidents "shall from time to time give to the Congress information of the state of the union and recommend to their consideration such measures as he shall judge necessary and expedient."

25th Amendment—One of 26 amendments (or changes) to the Constitution, this 1967 amendment made it clear that the vice president will serve as president if the president "is unable to discharge the powers and duties of his office." It also established a procedure for replacing a president who is too sick to continue as president (the vice president takes over), and a method of selecting a new vice president when the vice president becomes president, resigns, or dies.

Veto—Meaning "forbid." This is the power given to presidents to disapprove a new law approved by the Congress.

Vice president—Created by the Constitution, this is the second highest elected office in the United States.

White House—The official residence of the president as well as the best-known and most important building for a president's staff and facilities.

Further Reading

Corwin, Edward S. *The President: Office and Powers, 1787–1957*, 4th ed. New York: New York University Press, 1957.

McDonald, Forrest. *The American Presidency: An Intellectual History.* Lawrence, Kansas: University Press of Kansas, 1994.

Neustadt, Richard E. *Presidential Power and the Modern Presidents: The Politics of Leadership from Roosevelt to Reagan,* 2nd ed. New York: Free Press, 1990.

Olasky, Marvin. *The American Leadership Tradition: Moral Vision from Washington to Clinton.* New York: Free Press, 1999.

Patterson, Bradley H. Jr. *The Ring of Power: The White House Staff and Its Expanding Role in Government.* New York: Basic Books, 1988.

Skowronek, Stephen. *The Politics Presidents Make: Leadership from John Adams to George Bush.* Cambridge, MA: Harvard University Press, 1993.

Shenkman, Richard. *Presidential Ambition.* New York: HarperCollins, 1999.

ABOUT THE AUTHOR: Kevin J. McNamara is a former journalist and aide to a member of Congress. Today he serves as an assistant vice president of Drexel University and as an adjunct scholar of the Foreign Policy Research Institute.

SENIOR CONSULTING EDITOR Arthur M. Schlesinger, jr. is the leading American historian of our time. He won the Pulitzer Prize for his book *The Age of Jackson* (1945) and again for *A Thousand Days* (1965). This chronicle of the Kennedy Administration also won a National Book Award. Professor Schlesinger is the Albert Schweitzer Professor of the Humanities at the City University of New York, and has been involved in several other Chelsea House projects, including the REVOLUTIONARY WAR LEADERS and COLONIAL LEADERS series.

Picture Credits